CONTENTS

RIDDLES ARE SECRETS

A riddle is a secret with clues. When you tell a riddle, you're sharing the clues. And when you work out the answer, you can feel your brain growing. No one wants a tiny brain, do they? So help your friends and share a riddle!

PUZZLING RIDDLES

TO STUMP YOUR FRIENDS

MICHAEL DAHL

C016571957

Raintree is an imprint of Capstone Global Library Limited, a company incorporated in England and Wales having its registered office at 264 Banbury Road, Oxford, OX2 7DY – Registered company number: 6695582

www.raintree.co.uk
myorders@raintree.co.uk

Edited by Mandy Robbins
Picture research by Eric Gohl
Production by Tori Abraham

ISBN 978 1 4747 5472 9
22 21 20 19 18
10 9 8 7 6 5 4 3 2 1

British Library Cataloguing-in-Publication Data
A full catalogue record for this book is available from the British Library.

Acknowledgments
The author and publisher are grateful to the following for permission to reproduce copyright material:Shutterstock: Andrey_Kuzmin, 15, Balefire, 29, Bomshtein, 30 (left), evenfh, 20, EvgeniiAnd, 12 (bricks), Hogan Imaging, 17, Hong Vo, 30 (top), Hurst Photo, 21, Jan Martin Will, 18, jopelka, 10, Little Perfect Stock, 24, Maksim Shmeljov, 27, Muellek Josef, 9, Nerthuz, 23, nito, 12 (feathers), Offscreen, 8, Photoonlife, 7, PongMoji, 14, Portogas D Ace, 28, Pro3DArtt, 31, Stockforlife, 11, sumire8, 30 (right), Sundari, 31 (background), Vacclav, 26, vovan, 22

Printed and bound in India.

Follow these tips to get big laughs.

1. **Keep a straight face** when telling your riddle. You don't want to give anything away with your facial expressions.

2. **If your friends are stumped**, give them a clue. But don't make it too easy. You want them to think and work out the answer for themselves.

3. **When you say the answer**, say it clearly and loudly. Make it sound like a surprise! This will probably make your audience chuckle and enjoy it even more!

HA!

QUICK QUIZZERS

The most famous riddle is the Riddle of the Sphinx. It asks:

"What goes on four feet in the morning, two at noon, and three at night?"

Answer: **People!** At the start, or morning, of their lives, people crawl on all fours. At noon, the middle of life, they walk on two feet. At night, in old age, they walk with a walking stick, which gives them three feet.

1. What has two hands but no arms or legs?

A clock

1. What has a head and a foot
but no body?

Your bed

2. What gets wetter and wetter
the more it dries?

A towel

3. What has to be broken
before you can use it?
An egg

4. What building has
the most storeys?
The library

1. What falls but never breaks?

Night

2. What kind of room has no windows or doors?

A mushroom

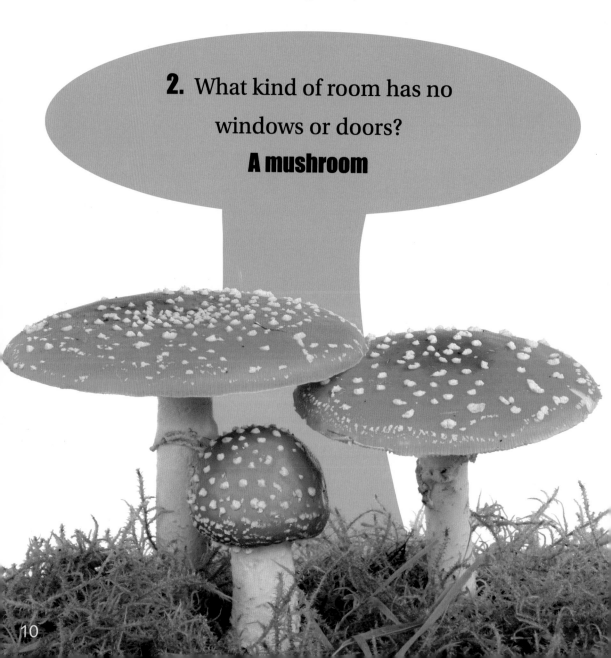

3. What is full of holes
but can still hold water?
A sponge

4. What do you call a fish
without an eye?
Fsh

5. What has four legs but
never moves?
A table

PUZZLING POSERS

LEVEL: MEDIUM

1. What two things can you never
eat for breakfast?
Lunch and dinner

2. What can travel around the world
but never leaves its corner?
A stamp

3. Which is heavier, a kilogram of bricks
or a kilogram of feathers?
Neither – they are exactly the same!

1. What can you catch but never
throw away?

A cold

2. What is at the end of a rainbow?

The letter W

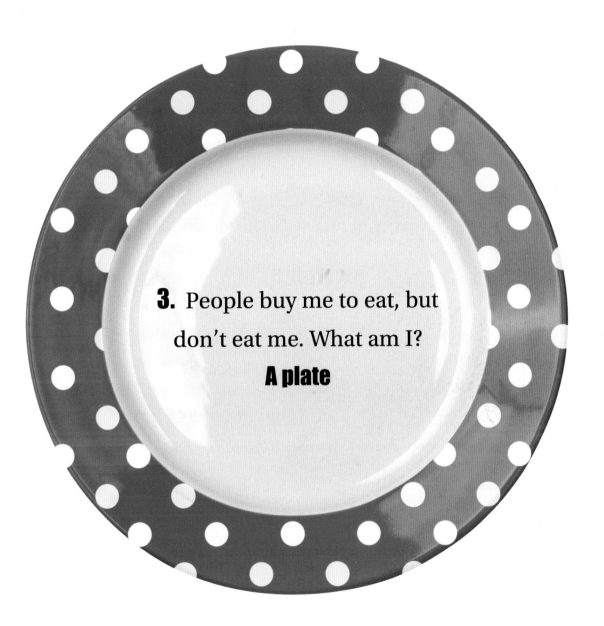

3. People buy me to eat, but don't eat me. What am I?

A plate

1. What is the only question where the answer is never "Yes"?

"Are you asleep?"

2. What word is spelled incorrectly in every dictionary?

"Incorrectly"

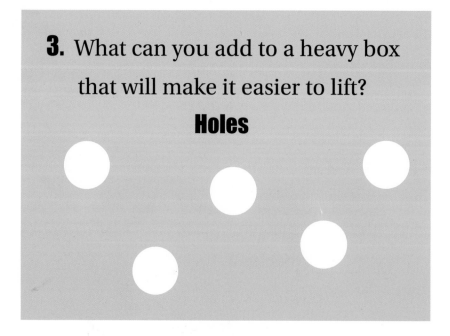

3. What can you add to a heavy box that will make it easier to lift?

Holes

4. Who is bigger: Mr Bigger,

Mrs Bigger, or their baby?

The baby, because he's a little Bigger

STUNNING STUMPERS

LEVEL: HARD

1. I'm light as a feather, yet the strongest man can't hold me for more than 5 minutes. What am I?

Your breath

2. Poor people have it. Rich people need it. If you eat it you die. What is it?

Nothing

3. What goes around and around a tree, but never gets tired?

The bark

1. No matter how hungry they may be, people in the Arctic will never eat a penguin. Why? **Because penguins live at the South Pole. The Arctic is in the North Pole.**

2. A king, a queen and two twins all lay in a large room. But there are no grown-ups or children in the room. How can this be?

They are different types of beds.

3. What is as big as Godzilla but doesn't weigh anything?

Godzilla's shadow

1. How many seconds are in a year?

Twelve! 2nd January,

2nd February, 2nd March...

Sun	Mon	Tue	Wed	Thu	Fri	Sat
1	(2)	3	4	5	6	7
8	9	10	11	12	13	14
15	16	17	18	19	20	21
22	23	24	25	26	27	28
29	30	31				

2. What ancient invention lets you look right through a wall?

A window

BOGGLING BRAIN-BUSTERS

LEVEL: GENIUS

1. Willie's mother has three children. The first is called April, the next is called May. What's the name of the third child?

Willie of course!

2. A cowboy rode into town on Friday. He stayed in town for three days and rode out on Friday. How was that possible?

Friday was the name of his horse.

1. Mr Blue lives in the blue house.

Mr Pink lives in the pink house.

Mr Brown lives in the brown house.

Who lives in the white house?

The US president

2. A boy was rushed to the hospital. But the doctor said, "I cannot operate on this boy. He is my son!" Yet the doctor was not the boy's father. How could this be?
The doctor was the boy's mother.

3. A lorry driver is going in the opposite direction of all the vehicles on the street. But the police don't stop him. Why?
He is walking.

1. You are in a dark cabin. You have only one match. There is a newspaper, a lamp, a candle and a fireplace. Which should you light first?

The match

2. Two girls were born to the same mother, on the same day, in the same year. But they aren't twins. How can this be?

The girls are two members of a set of triplets!

3. What starts with T, ends in T and only has T in the middle?

A teapot

1. Grandma is knocking at the door. She's come for breakfast, but you forgot! You have a jar of peanut butter, a jar of jam and a bag of bread. What do you open first?

The door – let Grandma in!

2. A man was outside walking in the rain. He didn't have an umbrella, a hat or a raincoat. His clothes and shoes got soaked. But not a hair on his head got wet. Why?

He was bald.

3. Where can you find a microwave?

On a teeny, tiny beach!

FIND OUT MORE

BOOKS

Roald Dahl Whoppsy-Whiffling Joke Book, Roald Dahl (Puffin, 2018)

The Everything Kids' Giant Book of Jokes, Riddles and Brain Teasers, Various Authors (Adams Media Corporation, 2010)

World's Best (and Worst) Riddles (Laugh Your Socks Off!), Georgia Beth (Lerner Classroom, 2018)

WEBSITES

www.activityvillage.co.uk/games
Activity Village

learnenglishkids.britishcouncil.org/en/fun-games
British Council